THE TAO TE CHING
AND THE CHRISTIAN WAY

THE TAO TE CHING

AND
THE CHRISTIAN WAY

A New English Version

Joseph Petulla

ORBIS BOOKS

Maryknoll, New York 10545

Copyright © 1998 by Joseph Petulla

Published by Orbis Books, Maryknoll, New York, U.S.A.

Manufactured in the United States of America.

Cover art by Rob Weinberg, a graphics and book designer in the coast side community of Pacifica, near San Francisco. You can visit his website at http:\\www.spindrift.org.

Art within the text from Wang Ch'i and Wang Ssu-i, *San-ts'ai t'u-hui* (China, 1610).

Library of Congress Cataloging in Publication Data

Petulla, Joseph.
    The tao te ching and the Christian way / Joseph Petulla.
      p. cm.
    ISBN 1-57075-211-7 (pbk.)
    1. Lao-tzu. Tao te ching. 2. Tao. 3. Christianity—Philosophy.
I. Title.
    BL1900.L35P47   1998
    299'.51482—dc21   98-35571

Contents

Preface

My Path to the Tao

In a small, cramped used bookstore more than a decade ago, I stumbled onto a slim paperback book with a large Chinese character on the cover. It was entitled *The Way of Life according to Lao Tzu*. I opened it at random and started to read. Soon I was sitting on the floor with my back against the bookshelf, completely engrossed in its powerful message. I read most of the book that day, took it home, and began to use it for morning meditation. From the beginning I was impressed that the contents, compiled in China from three to seven centuries before Christ, coincided remarkably with Christian theology and mysticism, and moreover, that it concentrated on the essentials of a lived religious life and a healthy spiritual outlook.

Since that day I have found and collected many translations of the book, some from meticulous Chinese scholars, others more interpretative versions from secondary sources, some fairly pompous and obscure, others more accessible. I have attempted my rendition mainly because I love the text, and I want to present an American version as clearly as possible; I also want to point out how easily it can be read as a very impressive Christian text.

Since I am not a scholar with Chinese language expertise, I have based my version on several older, literal translations by scholars and have tried to distill the essential meaning of each verse and chapter. And because I have been partial to that first translation I read by Witter Bynner, done in 1944, I have leaned heavily on it; I have also relied on the translation and comments by Raymond B. Blakney, a former Christian missionary and teacher in China, who was also a scholar and author of other books on Eastern religions. Bynner himself said he desired to do a new translation because he wanted to make *The Tao* more accessible to people of his generation. In that purpose I am imitating my Taoist mentor and can only hope that readers of this volume get as much out of my work as I did from his.

What is different about this edition is that I have tried to convey the powerful conjunction of Christian and Taoist themes through my reflections following each Taoist lesson, basing them on Christian scripture and spirituality and through my afterword: The *Tao Te Ching* and Christianity. Jesus said, "I am the Way, the Truth and the Life"; the Taoist *Way of Life* is an astonishing anticipation of a great number of his teachings and his pattern of life, written in a remote section of China centuries before his birth. Thus the purpose of this book is to show that a committed Christian can read this wonderful ancient text with great personal spiritual gain and fulfillment, thus the title *The Tao Te Ching and the Christian Way*.

Tao means "Way," or the "way" we should live our lives, and according to the *Tao Te Ching* it is the power within nature which guides that way or path. In the New Testament Jesus also reveals himself as a model and truth or "way" to live; moreover, he is the living source and power of all life in nature and humans. That is, Christians understand Jesus himself is the pattern of the law and way of life, present in the world today. This reality is the source of Christian faith, hope, and love. As the reader will discover, the *Tao Te Ching* presents a remarkable outline of how a Christian can live that life with simplicity, happiness, compassion, and love.

The Cover Art

I owe a debt of great gratitude to Rob Weinberg, who has done the cover of this book. Deeply identified with the Zen Buddhist tradition, Rob is imbued with an ecumenical spirit as well.

In the cover we are reminded that for Eastern thought, the moon is often regarded as far away and ungraspable, while at the same time it illuminates the world as the mild side of the sun. The moonlit landscape is subtle and unimposing, which is how Lao Tzu describes his *Tao* or "Way." Under the moon, the pathway is not distinct from the forest that surrounds it and — as both Lao and Jesus point out — the Way is something we must look for and discover as we live each day. East and West converge in spirituality as we seek and find the riches of the Way.

The stream is the second focus of the image, water running through the middle of the landscape, a symbol of life-giving power in both East and West. Water is a cleansing agent in the Tao, and it symbolizes the passage from the death of sin to life in Christ in Christianity.

The unobtrusive church at the bottom of the landscape reminds us that God is present in the world, both in God's people as they live their lives and in nature. That is a major focus of the *Tao Te Ching* of Lao Tzu, of the Way of Jesus, and of this book.

THE TAO TE CHING
AND THE CHRISTIAN WAY

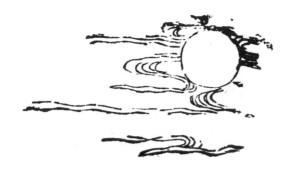

Life Is a Wondrous Mystery

Existence never presents itself
With perfect clarity.
Words are too frail to describe
The depth of its Reality.
Before heaven and earth came to be,
There were no words.
Words came from the womb of matter,
And whether we are looking
For the Spirit living in the world, or
Dazzled, see only the surface of things,
Spirit and surface remain
Essentially the same,
Though words seem to make them
Different, because they describe
Opposite experiences.
If you need to name all Reality,
Wonder describes both

Inside and outside.
Life opens to us
When we understand wonder.

Although as Christians we believe we live the life of Christ in the world, we can never penetrate the total truth of God's wisdom. Even Jesus himself cried out to his Father in Gethsemane to help him to understand and carry out his will. We can see only "the surface" of things and pray to God to be able to see "the inside" of his Reality. Wonder is our "Way of Life" because our lives "are the Lord's doing and marvelous in our eyes" (Matt 21:42).

Freedom of the Children of God

People tend to size up situations
And other people too quickly:
Beautiful-ugly,
Competent-incompetent, even
Living-dead,
Because life and death seem to show
The basic contradiction of existence.
We speak about what is difficult
And what is easy,
Long or short,
High or low,
And we think we've got it right.
But in truth, life is more like music,
With subtle differences in tone,
As what was becomes transformed
Into what is,
And what is into what will be.
The wise and healthy person
Doesn't think in categories
Or make absolute judgments, but
Accepts everything that happens
As it comes,
Not to possess an event,
But rather to breathe ourselves into it
And to work with it.
We should not want to own life,

But rather to sail with its breezes
Without arrogance or self-promotion.
If you do not assume importance,
You cannot lose it.

Christians live with the freedom of the children of God. That is, we feel free to live life as Jesus our brother shows it to us, rather than judging the world and those around us in black and white terms. Our inheritance as children of God allows us to freely participate in the complex symphony of life, breathing our contribution into creation, thus adding our notes of joy and suffering to the musical score. In Jesus' words we are the leaven that enlivens creation with no other effort but that of being ourselves, "because only a little leaven leavens the whole lump" (Gal 5:9).

3

Finding True Happiness

When prestige is offered for money,
Some people battle for it;
When glittering products are sold,
Others want to steal them;
Advertisers strive to make us
Covet their wares.
It is better for us
To find ways to open people's hearts,
Fill their stomachs,
Calm their dispositions,
To clarify for them what they really need,
So no charlatan can trick them
Into living a useless life.
People need to freely choose
The True and the Good.

As Christ lived a life of simplicity and service to others, so happiness for Christians is also found in the simplicity of service, not storing up treasures for ourselves or being duped by money and power, which undermine the foundations of the Way. Christ's example and words guide us to a life of helping and compassion, "where our true treasure and happiness are because that is where our hearts are" (Matt 6:21).

4

The Source of All Life

The Parent of the universe
Has no beginning and yet
Is the Source of all life.
It can round the sharpest edges,
Loosen the tightest knots,
Settle the dust of the whirlwind, as
A never-failing Provider to all beings.
But where in all the universe
Did this Begetter begin?

*In the beginning, says the Gospel of John, was the Word, or Way,
and all things came into being through that Way to show forth
the goodness of God. The Way remains the never-ending
provider for all creation, yet still makes us wonder where the
Greatest of all Great came from and why he should continue to
show everlasting kindness to the universe. His answer comes
through Jesus and creation itself, the living example of his love.*

5

Wonders of the Universe

Nature flourishes and decays
Without a second thought about it.
Humans are born, live, and die
Without a second thought about it.
The universe is like a gigantic bellows,
Forever emptying itself, forever expanding.
The more it gives up, the more it gains.
Humans go crazy arguing over these things,
And it would be enlightening for them
To look inside themselves for the answer.

We are sometimes overwhelmed by mysteries of life and death, of good and evil. Jesus told us that we need to look into ourselves with simplicity, teaching that his Father "concealed these things from the learned and wise, and revealed them to the simple" (Luke 10:21), who accept the world for what it is, an image of Jesus' life and death.

6

The Way Shows a Mother's Love

The breath of life
Is a mothering mystery
As it hovers and moves
Through the universe,
Giving birth to and nourishing
The seed that lives forever.
All beings draw from
The mystery of life.
The more they drink from it,
The more remains for others.

All life is born from God and is a mothering mystery. "For even though a woman may forget her sucking child, God will never forget you" (Isa 49:15), Isaiah says, emphasizing that life is just as much a mystery in what is visible as in what is invisible. Our confidence comes from our knowledge that the visible is connected to the invisible by a mother's love.

7

To Become Our True Selves

The universe cannot die
Because its Foundation and Power
Are infinite.
Therefore a healthy and wise person
Relies on this Presence
And does not assume importance
Or push himself away from
The Being that sustains him.
It is only by not acting as though
We are completely independent from it
That we can more and more
Become ourselves.

The Way is the pattern of God's presence in the universe in Christ, who sustains everything that happens on earth, good and bad, life and death. These facts are what make faith so necessary and so difficult. Without faith and trust, "not in the wisdom of men but in the power of God" (1 Cor 2:5), nothing in the world can ever make sense.

8

Blessed Are the Poor in Spirit

When we are at our best,
We serve as we go along.
Like water we seek our level
In the most ordinary way, and
We love to live close to the earth,
Trying to keep our motives pure
And our words truthful and
Compassionate, while allowing
Other people their own freedom to be.
In this climate businessmen can
Deal with clients fairly and
Politicians can serve the people.

Followers of Jesus, who is the Way, the Truth, and the Light, aspire to live in the way he lived and taught. We try to "live with humility and gentleness" (Eph 4:2), not puffing ourselves up, but rather being true to how we find ourselves. This is the Way of Jesus and the way of the earth, of air, and of water, which remain true to the way they exist in the world.

9

Physically and Spiritually Healthy

Driving ourselves too hard
Is like overstretching a bow
That eventually breaks down,
Or like oversharpening a knife
That becomes thin and dull.
Overreaching will never satisfy us,
Not even with a house full of treasure,
Because our souls become weary and restless.
We are brought to our knees
By ambition and pride.
We can lead a full, happy life
Only if we do it without stress,
Without competing with everything in sight.

Jesus is the Way of how to live, giving us both power and example to become more and more like him. His words and actions are the model of living without stress. Conscious of his life in God and aware of the frailty of human life, he understood that his personal energy depended on God, not on human achievement or glory. Jesus was "humble and lowly of heart" (Matt 11:29), showing us that pride and ambition lead to disaster, both physical and emotional.

The Key to Heaven

Can you open the gate of your mind
Wide to everything the world brings you?
Can you become as simple
As a child, in the freedom of
Accepting all of life's offerings
And at the same time maintaining
The responsibilities of maturity?
Can you warmly relate to all humans
With genuine love and mutuality?
Can you become heaven's partner
In the creation of a better world?
Will you let the wisdom of your heart
Guide the machinations of your mind?
If you can truly nourish our growing children,
If you can guide others without selfish demands,
If you can help people without their knowing it,
You have found the core of life.

*Spirituality East and West concentrates on everyday activities
inspired by the strength of the divine love of the Way. "Over all
things put on love" (Col 3:14). "This I pray, that your love may
abound" (Phil 1:9). Love for others brings inner freedom,
simplicity, responsibility, and caring. It is Jesus living in the
world through us.*

Martha and Mary

Look at a wheel and you will find
Spokes joined by a round, empty hub;
Look at a clay pitcher and you will find
The empty space that can hold water;
We need doors and windows in a house
As vacant spaces for light and movement.
In other words, emptiness serves us
As well as busy tools do.

The Way is not the humdrum of constant activity. Jesus praised Mary for just sitting and listening, while Martha busily took care of the needs of his listeners. We need sometimes to pause and listen, to open ourselves to the world in a spirit of emptiness, in the spirit of the world itself as it creates, dies, and lies fallow until it creates again.

The Peace of Christians

Colors can deceive,
Music can deafen,
Tastes can sour.
The fast pace of life
Can drive us to distraction,
And success cannot slow down
Our ambitious march to nowhere.
So the healthy and wise person
Will develop an inner sense
Of peace
Rather than relying
Only on external goals.
In this way we will find
The true road to joy.

*The fruits of living the Christian Way are ripened by union
with Jesus "in the Spirit and bond of peace" (Eph 4:3). "For the
wisdom from above is peaceable" (Jas 3:17). Peace represents the
inner quality of the Way no matter how active we find
ourselves. It is the gift that comes from "God filling us with joy
and peace in believing" (Rom 15:13).*

13

Success and Failure

To be an acclaimed celebrity
Can bring as many problems
As falling into disgrace.
Success can bring as much misery
As total failure.
How can celebrity status
Be as bad as disgrace?
For one thing, winning acclaim
Burdens a person with the fear
Of losing something everyone else covets.
How can success bring
As much misery as total failure?
Because we think that our personal worth
Is built only by material gain or loss.
When we stop thinking that our lives
Have no more value than glittering prizes,
Neither success nor failure can bother us.

Celebrity or disgrace, success or failure,
We must begin to understand that
All of us are members of the same Body
And share a common destiny.
Knowing this truth enables us
To set an example for one another.

The Way reorients our understanding of success and failure. People living an ordinary life in the world often think of success in a way that leads to turmoil and misery. Success for Christians is the "prosperity for those who hear and serve God" (Job 36:11) as present in the world. True success belongs to those who understand that, as humans, we "are the body of Christ" (Rom 12:5), and we are born into a community which shares a common destiny.

14

The Faith of Christians

When we look for something we cannot see
And call it invisible;
Listen for something we cannot hear
And say it is inaudible;
When we grasp for something we cannot reach
And call it unreachable;
All these experiences of reaching out
But not attaining
Are symbols of an elusive Oneness
That not only rises into sunlight
Or sets into darkness
But also issues forth a stream
Of living beings as incomprehensible
As the Eternal Power to which they return.
That is why so many people
Do not believe the Eternal is real.
Life has no meaning, they say.
Existence is a cruel joke
Inflicted upon us by chance, they say.
There is no There there,
No sustaining Life beyond ourselves.
Yet those of us who become aware of
The eternal Power, Presence, and
Essence in our everyday life
Know ultimate Truth each moment,
Because true Life flows both inside
And outside of time.

"Faith is the assurance of things hoped, the certainty we cannot see" (Heb 11:1). Religion itself is belief in an invisible world governed by an all-powerful Being. Because we have no visible proof for what we believe, "We walk by faith, not by sight" (2 Cor 5:7) and thus are tested to live according to our beliefs. The object of our faith is an elusive mystical oneness, to which we must return day by day for nourishment and strength.

The Sayings of Jesus

Ever since ancient times
Human tradition has collected
A body of wisdom, and some of it
Has come down to us in the form of
Sayings, such as:
"Alert as a person walking on thin ice."
"Wary as a stranger in a notorious neighborhood."
"Considerate as a welcoming host."
"Selfless as melting ice."
"Green as a young tree in the spring."
"Open as a deep river valley."
And this one: "Turbulent as a rushing stream."
Why "Turbulent as a rushing stream?"
Because when we are upset,
How can we calm down
Unless we are patient enough
To wait for the stream to flow more slowly,
So the mud can settle and
The water can clarify itself?
How can we know the direction
Our lives should take unless
We let ourselves flow with the current
Without trying to control every turn?
When we learn how to allow life
To take its own quick or languid pace,
We find that we need only
This Force to keep us well energized.

Shocks pass through us.
We feel no wear or tear.

Many of the gospel teachings are made up of "sayings" of Jesus, similar to the ones mentioned above. One speaks of patience as waiting for the mud to settle out of the water, in Christian terms as "walking with patience and forbearance in love" (Eph 4:2). A central message of the earliest Christians was "to be patient until the Lord's coming" (Jas 5:7). These suggestions of the Tao remind us that we cannot control everything in our lives. We must learn to be less controlling, to let go, to wait for Jesus to show us the Way.

The Mystery of Life and Death

Know the simple roots of your life
And you will possess the key to peace.
Understand that we share life
With everything growing and blooming
Until together we return to our quiet origins,
Just as a beautiful flower grows, dies,
And becomes one with the earth.
Some people say that total acceptance
Of the cycle of life is passive quietism,
Or, worse, a destructive fatalism.
Actually it shows a deep understanding
Of destiny, facing up to the facts of life,
Rather than living with blinders on.
When you open your eyes,
You open your mind;
When you open your mind,
You open your heart;
When you open your heart,
You live with dignity;
When you live with dignity,
You share divine life;
When you share divine life,
You can build a community of love;
When you build a community of love,
You enter eternity;
When you enter eternity,
Nothing can harm you;

When nothing can harm you,
You will live forever,
Even now in this present moment.

*The heart of Christianity is sharing in the life and death of
Christ, which is one with the dying and rising of all of nature.
We are born, grow, and mature, then begin to die in our physical
bodies. Yet in our spiritual lives we are dying to selfishness and
rising in grace every day as we share in the life of Christ's body
on earth. "We know we have passed from death to life because
we have loved the brethren" (1 John 3:14).*

The Selflessness of Love

We help people best
When they don't realize they are being helped.
Rather than acting to show ourselves off
Or to induce return favors and gratitude,
We need to cultivate a deep respect for others,
With the same kind of love we need ourselves.
In helping others it is better not to say much,
So when we act generously,
People will feel ennobled, not degraded.

The gospel says, "Do not love only those who love you, for even sinners love those who love them" (Matt 5:46). Our love is based on the selfless love of Jesus, who "loved us and gave himself up for us" (Eph 5:2), not because we proved ourselves worthy of his love. Yet as the Tao indicates, our love is, unfortunately, too often based on what we can get out of it.

Freedom from the Law

Because people often do not choose
To live their everyday lives
With respect for one another,
Laws are written to require
Honesty, fairness, and justice.
Official learning and official charity
Breed official hypocrisy.
When families cannot nurture love,
They begin to demand obedience.
When citizens do not have regard for one another,
They demand officers to keep the peace.

St. Paul distinguishes the state of freedom in Christ from servitude under the law; we are "released from the law" (Rom 7:6) because Christ's death and resurrection ushered in the new life of love, a life not based on obedience to commandments but on love for one another. "Everyone who believes is freed from all things" (Acts 13:39) in the sense that love is our common way of life, not obedience to the law. The Way of Jesus is both the goal and the power to achieve the goal.

Living without Baggage

We could throw out
Most formal learning and public knowledge,
And we would be far happier.
If parents did not discipline their children so
Harshly, their families would share more love.
When we outlaw legalized profiteering,
We will be rid of most thievery in the world.
Public life has lost its purpose.
If we really want people
To become happy and free,
We will show them how to live
Without greedy ambitions or wanton luxuries.

When Jesus threw the moneychangers out of the Temple, he was justly angered by their exploitation of the faith for profit, and also by a disfiguring of daily life into a faith based on money. "Do not make my Father's house a house of merchandise" (John 2:16). So much of our own learning and politics is directed to money-making purposes. "Things are in the saddle," said Emerson, and it is our job to see to it that money and things do not take charge of our hearts.

Uses of Knowledge

What good is education
If we learn only abstract distinctions
That apply neither to life nor to science?
What good are mental generalizations
If they merely stereotype other people
And set up silly propositions, like
"If one person leads,
Another must follow."
This is untrue and nonsense.
Of course, it is easier
To lead a conventional life,
To follow the crowd blindly.
Personally, I am a ne'er-do-well,
To others I am a childish fool,
Homeless, the lowest of the low.

How worthless I must seem,
With no worldly goods,
While others swim in luxuries.
What a fool I am, how stupid
Not to be able to make my way in life.
Most people are so confident, so proud,
While I thrash about pitifully like a dying fish.
Yet I drift along and should be miserable
While other people concentrate on
Making their mark.
Oh well, I guess I am just different,
A perpetual infant nursing at the breast.

Jesus makes a distinction between knowledge that furthers the good and love of the world, and the knowledge that blocks love. He said, "Alas for you lawyers. You have taken away the key of knowledge. You did not use it yourself, and those who would have used it, you stopped" (Luke 11:52). We know the key of knowledge to be that which leads to love and caring among members of the community, not knowledge that leads to division, hate, and war. Like Jesus, the author of this lesson says he is an object of scorn for his life and beliefs.

The Will of God

One certain way to find out
If we are spiritually healthy
Would be to ask ourselves
If we can accept everything life has to offer,
Good and bad, pleasure and pain,
Without demanding to know why,
Without needing an explanation
For every confounding episode that besets us.
Life's struggles are born from that
Inexplicable, awesome Wellspring
Of all that happens in the world,
That hides in the darkness of mystery,
And its deepest reasons can never be known.
This Power is as far away
As the most distant star,
And as near to us as the tip of our nose.
Thus has it been from all eternity.
Do we need to know
More about life and death than this?

As Christians we seek to follow "the mystery of God's will" (Eph 1:9) by accepting life's duties and living the love of Jesus in the world. "Thy will be done," we pray in the Lord's Prayer, knowing that "this is the will of God, your sanctification" (1 Thess 4:3). All we need to know is that we should share Christ's love with everyone we meet and abide in that love in spite of everything negative that happens to us in the world. God's will is that which is right in front of our noses.

Living the Life of Christ

When we give in to a shock,
Its impact is weakened.
When we are ready for anything,
We are not surprised when it happens—
Good or bad!
When we keep our mind and heart open,
We can absorb the richness of life.
If we know how to accept pain,
We heal much faster.
And just as poverty can mature us,
Wealth can bewilder and belittle.
Knowing these things, a spiritually
Healthy person develops an
Attitude everyone respects.
Without getting excited, we come to life;
Without trying to justify ourselves,
We are justified;
Without trying to take credit for anything,
We are given credit for the way we live;
Without making claims for ourselves,
We live a life of satisfaction;
And because we don't compete for anything,
We enjoy peace of mind.
How true is the old saying,
"Give in to a shock and its impact is weakened."
How true it is!

Christians share in the life of Jesus on earth. This means that we share his pain and loss as well as his joy and triumphs. "Christ had to suffer and rise again" (Acts 17:3). "Since Christ suffered, arm yourself with the same mind" (1 Pet 4:1). We realize that life is filled with hardships, but we are strengthened as we live it in union with the deepest presence of Jesus. Pain can be real but not lasting because we know all things are "like grass sprouting in the morning and withering by evening" (Ps 90:6). Christ is forever.

Living the Way with Joy

Nature does not have to make an issue
Of anything it does.
It can blow and shower
For as long as it has the energy,
Then stop. It's natural.
If nature does not make an issue
Of anything, why should we?
It's natural to follow the Way,
So when we practice it,
We feel truly alive and blessed.
When we abandon it, we feel lost.
When we are loyal to the Way,
We are comfortable with ourselves and others.
When we abuse it, we feel abused.
When we gladly show respect for others,
We ourselves are made worthy of respect.

The beauty of nature is its clarity. It does what it does, sustained by the same Spirit that supports us all. "The fruit of this Spirit is joy" (Gal 5:22). Living the Way should be primarily a life of joy, one that knows pain yet also experiences all the wonders of life that lift our spirits. "The disciples were filled with joy and with the Holy Spirit" (Acts 13:52).

Character of Christians

If we stand on our tip-toes,
We soon lose our balance;
Without a sense of rhythm,
We don't keep a steady pace;
When we try too hard to inspire,
We lose our ability to convince;
When we are too self-absorbed,
No one pays attention to us;
When we are too self-admiring,
People turn away from us.
Pride quenches any social value
We might wish for ourselves,
And it disgusts our neighbors and friends,
So a spiritually healthy person,
Living the Way, will shake off
All prideful living and selfish desires.

The early Christians, following their Master, were known for their "humility and gentleness" (Eph 4:2). These characteristics have been the goal of all those who follow the Way, that is, not regarding others with pride or arrogance, but rather imitating Jesus who "emptied himself for others" (Phil 2:7). For Christians, living for others is the same as living with nature.

The Creation of All Things

Before anything was created,
A Presence existed,
Complete and self-contained in every way,
Unchanging and without form
Or material expression of any kind,
Yet embodying the beautiful quality
Of unending motherhood.
Nothing of such magnificence
Could ever have a suitable name,
But I have called it "The Way of Life."
Maybe it should be called
"The Fullness of Life,"
Since fullness implies something
Eternal, ever-widening into space,
Creating a completed circle.
In this sense heaven and earth
Are fulfilled in the Way
That enables the rest of us to be made whole.
These are the four aspects of fulfillment
In the universe, and we are one of them:
We fulfill the Way of the earth,
The earth fulfills the Way of heaven,
And heaven fulfills all things,
Completing the full circle.

However we describe the creation of the world, we see that we must have greatness in us because the universe itself is so amaz-

*ingly great. "Through the Word [Way], all things were made"
(John 1:3). We fulfill the plan of creation because we are Christ's
brothers and sisters, and he "is the beginning of God's creation"
(Rev 3:14). Only through the Way (the Word) can creation be
fulfilled and can we live up to our incredible destiny in the
universe.*

The Road to Emmaus

Life is like a walk in the woods;
We don't mindlessly run through it.
Even if we are traveling
And need to move along,
We should slow down enough
To enjoy the beauty of our surroundings.
No general is so foolish as to move
Too far ahead of his supply train
And risk losing his army and the battle.
Life should be a matter
Of mild pacing and graceful living.

The two disciples walking on the road to Emmaus (Luke 24:13–32) after the resurrection provide an image of Christians walking through life. Like them we are sometimes so caught up in the excitement of events around us that we cannot slow down enough to recognize Jesus walking with us. When we stop, share a meal with others, and see Jesus in our midst, we can appreciate "the signs and wonders in the power of the Spirit" (Rom 15:19) in our everyday lives. We need to slow down to be able to smile and enjoy.

Sharing Talent and Virtue

Mature people often have many qualities
In common with the immature.
For example, either group can
Speak flawlessly with perfect diction,
Or calculate numbers with precision,
Or construct perfect doors and windows,
And tie beautiful, tight knots.
Yet if mature people want to help
The immature, they must recognize that
They also possess many of the same qualities
Of immaturity that they see in others.
If they don't understand this lesson
Of nature, they are as far off
The mark as the immature people
They want to help.
That is the heart of the matter.

*Christians think of themselves as special, as "a city set on a hill,"
apart from others in our beliefs and way of life. Our understanding of the Way and life in Christ is different, but we are
not so different from others in our talents and frailties. "Our
bodies are sown in weakness and raised in power" (1 Cor
15:43); all of us under the sun are equal in faults and virtues. It
is the love of Christ that empowers us to serve others, not our
own virtue.*

We Create the World

All men and women are endowed
With an amazing creative ability
That transforms our humble daily activities
Into images of shadows and light,
Which are infused into the world and
Impressed onto other worldly beings.
All of us—the high and the low—
Are the continuous conductors
Of the Source of all life, touching
One another with the unending
Life of creation.

We all have the ability to change the world around us by the way we work and live. The early Christians had a profound impact on those around them because "they were devoted to one another in brotherly love" (Rom 12:10) and "to the priestly service of the gospel" (Rom 15:16). If all people affect others by their actions, Christians influence people around them with the special character of Christ's own love.

True Power and Strength

There will always be people
Who try to take over the world
And shape it for their own purposes,
But they never succeed.
The earth is too sacred
To be grasped by the profane,
So it will slip from their grasp
At their first touch.
For a short time the corrupt can win.
Sometimes they can push others aside,
They can shout down the timid,
They can enrich themselves
While others go hungry,
They can keep the world's goods for themselves
And despoil the wondrous gifts of nature, but
The spiritually healthy are not fooled by the foolish.
They do not desire power,
Do not overextend themselves,
Do not exhaust themselves,
Do not see themselves above
The precious world around them.

Just as Christians do not place themselves above Christ or their brethren, they should not see themselves as above other brethren of the world they live in. The Christian ideal is one of "emptying oneself" (Phil 2:7), not lording over any person or creature in the world. Jesus' mission was "to bring down rulers and exult the humble" (Luke 1:52). "Whoever exults himself will be humbled and whoever humbles himself will be exulted" (Matt 23:12).

30

Those Who Live by the Sword

Followers of the Way know instinctively
That force of arms is a deadly game.
Weapons often turn on the users;
Every country wastes its youth on an army,
Whose purposes always lead to death.
Leaders and generals who engage in wars
To fight off tyrants and madmen,
First must know how to remove them
Without killing half the population,
How to lead with a cool head,
When passions and pride cloud the mind.
War is always a last resort, to be waged
To save the innocent and helpless.
Force solves no problems.
Life should be permitted to ripen like fruit
Before it falls to the ground.
If we live by the sword,
We are already dead.

Jesus' fundamental attitude toward violence was shown in Mark 14:43–48: "The crowd armed with swords and clubs surrounded him, and he said, 'have you come with swords and clubs to arrest me'?" He could have roused his followers and fought his enemies many times, but "the Lord does not deliver by sword or spear" (1 Sam 17:47), only by his love that "surpasses all understanding" (Eph 3:19).

Effects of War

No matter how dazzling and efficient
The weapons of war appear to be,
They are an evil, like the Black Death,
At whose beckon soldiers waste a useful life.
Good people risk corrupting a civilized
Humanity, brutalizing it by force of arms,
Which demonize their users.
Only the most serious reasons
Can justify the use of death-dealing
Instruments of war, only the last resort,
Accepted sadly by people and nations.
Winning is not a beautiful act.
Anyone who thinks so is
A person with a bloodthirsty heart,
And the bloodthirsty never
Prevail in the end.
It is always better to foster our
Sense of goodness and humanity,
Much worse to give in to base instincts,
When the young are sent out
To fight the wars of the old.
The nation at war is conducting a funeral
For their young, a time when everyone
Has cause to mourn.
Even when we win, all of us lose.

Christianity's relationship to war has been mixed. In the beginning early Christians refused to fight in Rome's wars of conquest and died for that belief. Over the years the Christian state has fought wars, just and unjust, in the name of Jesus, despite his pacifist message of love for all people. Christians likewise have assumed for themselves Jesus' message of "peacemakers" not "war makers." "We have been given the ministry of reconciliation" (2 Cor 5:18–19), says St. Paul, not of warmongering.

Our Common Destiny

Living our lives is not as easy
As carving a block of wood,
Which we can set aside
When we get tired of working on it.
Life is a gift that influences everyone
Around us, and when we follow the
Way, it is hallowed and beautiful.
We strengthen one another, and
Heaven and earth are transformed
Into the freshness of spring and excitement,
Giving us the freedom to become
As wondrous as we can be. But
Class hatreds, ethnic strife, and racial divisions
Wipe out that harmony of living
And have a way of compounding their evils.
Only when healthy people decide
To heal the world around themselves
Through the power of the Way
Can we restore the glory of our existence.
All of us are like small streams
Who ultimately will meet in the one eternal sea.

Christians "pursue peace with all men" (Heb 12:14), following "Jesus the mediator of a new covenant" (Heb 9:15) who healed divisions among all manner of ethnicities, classes, races, and nations. The weapons inspired by the Way are "weapons with divine power" (2 Cor 10:4), the love to build bridges, heal strife, and bring enemies together as friends. Hatred is antithetical to the very notion of Christian living.

33

Jesus the Model

It is better to develop wisdom within ourselves
Than to scrutinize and judge others.
It is better to master our own waywardness,
Than to try to control other people.
If we are content with our own lives
We will avoid the frenzy of ambition.
The Way builds a life
That never will die.

Jesus is the simple model of our daily conduct: compassion, love, and service rather than using others for our own ends and worldly ambitions. "Whoever says he abides in him should walk as he walked" (1 John 2:6). "As you received Christ, so live in him" (Col 2:6). This is the meaning of the Way.

34

Love of Nature

Throughout the existence of the world
Nature has made no distinctions
When offering its bountiful gifts.
Grass, trees, insects, animals, humans:
All have partaken of its fullness
With not a murmur from Mother Nature.
She doesn't boast of her wonders,
Doesn't withhold anything of herself,
Doesn't complain about a lack of respect
And the many ravages to her body.
She is our perfect host, the foundation
Of civilization and life. How horribly
Humanity behaves toward her!

Christianity does not replace nature; it imitates its goodness in giving gifts to all, allowing everyone to take a share, and not even complaining when it is ravaged into waste and destruction. "Grace builds on nature," Christian theology teaches. We cannot live or love without the gifts God gives us through our own nature and the natural world. We continue God's love by respecting and loving all of nature, which he created for us.

35

Joy of the Christian

When a person is spiritually healthy,
We can see the Way impressed on the face,
So we feel relaxed and comfortable in its presence,
Just as we would feel warmth
In the home of a close friend.
It's an unforgettable sensation of joy,
Like waiting for a wonderful meal
With happy companions
At a family celebration.

The people of God "were joyful for all God had done" (2 Chron 7:10). Joy is the response of people who understand the blessings of creation and of God's goodness to them. "The fruit of the Spirit is joy" (Gal 5:22), exclaims St. Paul to his converts over and over again In short, "The kingdom of God itself is joy in the Holy Spirit" (Rom 14:17). This joy provides our lives with a sense of completion and meaning.

36

Confidence in God

If we feel vulnerable,
We once must have been attacked,
If we feel we need to protect ourselves,
We once must have been aggressive,
If we feel insulted,
We once must have felt power,
If we feel deprived,
We once must have had privilege.
Therefore a spiritually healthy person
Knows that humility serves us best.
The virtue befits our place in the world
And leads to peace of mind.

Our anxieties and insecurities sometimes weigh us down, and we become upset or aggressive in our daily life. "Martha was worried about many things" (Luke 10:40) and went to Jesus to tell him to ask her sister to help her. Jesus answered, "Martha, Martha, you are fussing about so many things. Only one thing is necessary" (vv. 41–42). The "one thing" is placing our confidence in God while living the divine life of the Way.

37

First Be, Then Do

It is better to live by being,
By showing forth the Way in ourselves,
Than by piling up thousands of
Mindless activities and speeches.
It is the Way that keeps everything
Centered in the Core, not our own
Plans and actions we consider good deeds.
Through the power of the Way we can muzzle
Our desire to acquire, possess, and control.
Thus does peace come to us quietly
And effortlessly from beyond ourselves.

Christian priorities focus first of all on God's glory and living in his grace, then on living his Way. "Think of the lilies of the field," Jesus said. "They don't work themselves up over nothing. . . . If God takes care of the grass in the field . . . how much more will he clothe you. Don't worry. These are the things unbelievers run after. No, concentrate on the kingdom, and all the rest will come to you as well" (Luke 12:27–31). The Way is God's kingdom.

38

Our True Well-Being

If we know we are healthy,
We stay healthy
Without making a fuss about it,
But if we are not sure we are healthy
And tell everyone we are healthy,
We will become unhealthy.
When we are healthy, we don't have
To stress the point or profit from it.
It's the same with kind people;
They don't try to figure out ways
To profit from their kindness.
It's different with other types of people.
For example, those who stress justice
Operate with a calculator mentality,
Always figuring the legal angles
To make a buck from others.
Or some people can be mean-spirited and
Will prosecute anyone who might make
The slightest misstep across their paths.
When we lose the Way of Life
We tend to go from bad to worse;
We lose decency, fairness, and honesty
Because we are consumed with how
We can improve our own lot.
People of wisdom root themselves
In the Way so that their lives
Bloom as glorious as beautiful flowers.

Scripture stresses the human tendency toward selfishness and egoism: "People will be lovers of self" (2 Tim 3:2), promoting our own ends; "everyone looks to his own things" (Phil 2:21); "where there is selfish ambition, there is disorder" (Jas 3:16). Sometimes we even convert our compassion into a way to make ourselves look good. St. Paul reminds us that love is patient, kind, envies no one, is never boastful or conceited or selfish or quick to take offense. Most of all it will never come to an end (1 Cor 13:4–8).

39

It All Goes Together

The circle of life can be seen in parts:
The heavens show forth clarity,
The earth, evident in its solidity,
Innocence, in the spirit,
In the valley, emptiness,
In the river, fertility,
The people and their leaders exist so that
They may serve the common good.
The heavens would be clouded without clarity,
The earth would crumble without solidity,
The spirit would fail without innocence,
The valley could not be filled without emptiness,
The river could not carry life without fertility,
The nation will die without the people.
The lowly always carry the leaders of the nation,
Becoming their roots and foundation,
So the leaders should serve the people
With humility, gratitude, and the

Openness of a wheel's hub.
The hub holds the spokes and the wheel
That allows a leader to drive the chariot.

*There is a marvelous completeness to the world and the kingdom
of God: "Jesus ascended that he might fill all things" (Eph 4:10).
The earth is material but suffused with and kept in being by the
life and power of God. "The whole earth is filled with his glory"
(Ps 72:19). Humans are also material, but "the church is the
fullness of him who fills all in all" (Eph 1:23). There is a unity
to life and the world that explains the Way in all its forms.*

40

The Circle of Life

All living beings are born, flourish,
Die, and return to the mist.
Their exuberance returns to quiet;
All people and things return to the state
Of never needing to exist in the world.

Christianity is a religion of death to life. Even as we live, we die to selfishness and sin, and we live in the life of Jesus, the Way. "If I ascend to the heavens, you are there; if I make my bed in hell, behold, you are there too" (Ps 139:8). Whether we are young or old, rich or poor, good or bad, all humans pass through the pains of living and death into the glories of earth and heaven.

Steadfast Living

Strong people, knowing the Way of Life,
Stay committed to it.
Weak people, knowing the Way of Life,
Live it according to their moods.
Stupid people, knowing the Way of Life,
Ignore it, complain about it, laugh at it.
They show their stupidity by their complaints:
"It is not for real."
"It holds back progress."
For them everything is backward,
Top turns upside down,
A level path becomes steep,
White looks black,
A full meal is not enough,
Stability becomes weakness,
Simplicity becomes a wilted flower.
But eternity is for people who know that
Life writes straight with crooked lines,
Strength is theirs who can feel beyond touch,
Harmony is theirs who can hear beyond sound,
Beauty is theirs who can see beyond the surface,
Life is theirs who can understand beyond words.
Our full measure of fulfillment.

*Daily life so uproots the tree of our faith that it takes special
effort and confidence in God "to hold fast in our faith and stand
firm in confidence" (Heb 3:5–14). St. Augustine wrote a treatise*

on the difficulties of "loving and enduring to the end," "gaining strength by loving the Way and persevering," and "continuing in the faith, stable and steadfast" (Col 1:23). Jesus told us his Way is not always easy, but the burden is light.

42

Rich and Poor

In the beginning there was one,
two, and three: Heaven, earth, and
Humans—existing in perfect balance.
There was the warm day and the cool night
For all who lived and died.
The lowly came, and then came
The high and mighty, who saw their
Power as right and proper because
"With the low there must be the high."
Yet ancient teachings say that
Those who reach for the top and
Use force to attain it will die the death.
We all know in our heart of hearts
That this is true.

A perennial problem of the ages is the relationship of rich and poor, especially the duties of the rich toward the poor. The first injunction of Jesus is that we should "not lay up treasures on earth" (Matt 6:19), and that "it is hard for the rich to enter the kingdom of God" (Matt 19:23). Those who follow the Way realize how rich they are in their gifts from God. Their wealth therefore is regarded as supporting a life of love for others.

43

Daily Problems

When a stream strikes a hard rock in the water,
It quickly yields and flows on;
Thus to solve the hardened difficulties
Of our lives we also should yield to them
And flow onward, for we can then return
At a better time to reassess our trials.
But this is a most difficult lesson
To learn and live by.

The "thorns that make our paths difficult to walk" (Hos 2:6) are common to those who walk in the Way. Jesus taught us to focus on the Way and not on the hindrances. "In him who loves the Way there is no cause for stumbling" (1 John 2:10), because those who love continue on the path without trying to smooth over every bump before they go on. Hard rocks or pains of life do not claim their attention, only the glory of the Way, because temporary difficulties define the nature of life itself.

44

Priorities of the Way

Which is more dear to you,
You or your reputation?
Which means more to you,
You or your possessions?
What is obviously more valuable
If it were lost?
When seen in the light of eternity,
Meanness is an abomination,
Niggardliness is silly, and so on.
We know good and bad.
We shouldn't be ashamed
To change our lives,
To start over again.
Over and over again.

"He that is in you is greater than he that is in the world" (1 John 4:4), St. John told the early Christians. He who supports our very being is more important than reputation, possessions, our pride, or status in society. We need to continually reassess our priorities as human beings and as Christians.

45

Unfinished Work

We never finish our work
Here on earth, however good
Everything seems in our lives.
As long as the truth is derided,
As long as people oppress one another,
Prophets are shouted down,
Statesmen are ignored and pushed aside,
We will need to calmly do our work.
We will run to get warm,
Sit in the shade to cool down,
And eventually things will get better.
We hope for the best.

"The Father living in me does his works" (John 14:10), Jesus told his disciples. And Jesus continues his work in the world through his disciples, as St. Paul repeated often to the early Christians, "the good deeds God has prepared us to do" (Eph 2:10). Like the author of the Tao, the Lord at the end times tells his disciples, "I have not found your works completed" (Rev 3:2). We live the Way knowing we can never be finished with the work of the Lord.

46

The Way and Its Opposite

In a land where the Way of Life is understood,
Cannons are converted into plowshares.
In a land where the Way of Life is not understood,
Young students are drafted into the military.
Money worship leads to weeping,
Money grasping leads to poverty,
Takeovers are the order of the day.
Wall Street replaces the Way.

Jesus tells us, "Where your treasure is, there will be your heart also" (Matt 6:21). When our treasure lies in warring or only in money, we lose the Way and find a life of deep unhappiness. "The treasures of wisdom and knowledge are hidden in Christ our Way" (Col 2:3), while the selfish seeking of power and money lead to personal disaster.

47

Seeking Jesus

We don't have to stand on the
Highest mountain or tallest building
To see and understand better, only
Return to the center of our being.
We cannot learn more about life
Outside the core of our existence,
We know this from our own experience.
At bottom, to do is to be.

The gospel tells the story of the "people who went in search of Jesus, and when they found him, they pressed him not to leave them" (Luke 4:42). We often seek the divine in out-of-the-way places, but we need to realize that we live in him everywhere. "Here is the test by which we can make sure that we are in him: whoever claims to be dwelling in him, binds himself to live as Christ himself lived" (1 John 2:5–6). This life is the core of our existence.

48

The Goal of Knowledge

Life is more important than knowledge.
Knowledge is good insofar as it enhances
Our understanding of life, and
Our living of the Way of Life.
The world precedes knowledge, and
We should lose ourselves living
In a way that enhances all being.
If we push at the world in an arrogant way,
It will push back in a catastrophic way.

Knowledge is not an end in itself. Instinctively we know that living is more important than knowing: "If I have all knowledge and have not love, I am nothing" (1 Cor 13:2), for "knowledge puffs up but love builds up" (1 Cor 8:1). The Way is the life of using knowledge for good, our own good and the good of others. Jesus did not emphasize knowing; he emphasized loving.

49

Fools for Christ's Sake

If we would know the Way,
We would open our hearts to everybody.
We would find good people good,
And even find bad people good
If our hearts were opened wide.
We would trust liars
As well as honest men, I think,
If we were good enough.
We would feel the heart-beats of others
Above our own, as difficult as that is
To imagine.

Throughout the Bible the fool is derided as one who does not believe, who reviles God, who builds his house upon the sand. But the prophets are called fools (Hos 9:7), and St. Paul tells us, "We are fools for Christ's sake" (1 Cor 4:10). That is because Christians are told to love their enemies and reject the security and pleasures the world says we should love.

50

Where Is Thy Sting?

Death seems to be the main issue of life
Since three out of ten die at birth.
Yet knowing this fact does not stop
The multitudes from giving birth, so
Determined they are to add to their numbers.
What is more astonishing is that there is
One out of ten who is so full of life, they say,
That even wild tigers and rhinos avoid him,
And their claws and horns do not know where
To injure him, nor do weapons of war
Know where to kill him.
How can this be?
Because he has no death to die.

The Christian's relationship to death is changed from that of inevitability and dread, "naked from the womb, and so departs" (Eccles 5:15), to one of the victory and joy of resurrection. "Death cannot separate us from the love of God" (Rom 8:38–39), because in the world we "have already died with Christ and our life is hid with his" (Col 3:3). With this confidence we should also be able to face wild tigers and rhinos.

51

Meaning of Gratitude

Life brought us into the world,
And strength has been given to us,
Though all of us have been given
Different shapes, sizes, and colors,
Even plants and animals of the field,
So that all living beings owe to their
Existence a grateful obedience,
Not forced but freely offered.
And since we are given this
Gift of life and the strength to
Eat and drink, work and play,
So we should imitate the Power
That lets us live.
We should act like parents not officers,
Servants not masters, concerned with
Nurturing precious lives,
Not demanding strict obedience.

Then we will abide in harmony
With Life itself.

The most fundamental ethical impulse is a positive response to goodness and value. Thus all religious faiths automatically want to give thanks to God for all the goodness shown to us in our lives: for the beauty and diversity and goodness of nature and fellow humans, for good fortune and health. The whole world "overflows with thanksgiving" (Col 2:7). "Thanks be to God for his inexpressible gift" (2 Cor 9:15), exclaims St. Paul about living life in Christ.

Learning about God

The source of Life serves us
Like a mother. We love both
Mother and children, yet know
We should learn about our Mother
More and more perfectly, and
Then death will lose its sting.
If we can curb our tongues and
Senses, we will avoid trouble.
When we live without discipline,
Nothing can protect us from ourselves.
We need to learn that we can study
Even the smallest details of the world
With insight, and can assist
The least desirable people
With tenderness, using the deepest
Treasures of our being. In this way
We can touch eternity.

The earth is our mother in giving us the gifts of life. She also provides us with "the light of the knowledge of the glory of God" (2 Cor 4:6). All life gives us "knowledge of God's mystery, that is, Christ" (Col 2:2), thus all things in life should interest us, give us joy, inspire us to love. It is so much more fulfilling to get up in the morning with joy when we are eagerly waiting to see God's face in the world.

Road Away from the Way

If I knew a good road to get to
My destination, would I lose it
Every time I made a turn?
Yet many people refuse to try
The one road that can lead us
To the most important goal of life.
Look at the lavish suburbs built
Far away from impoverished ghettos.
Hungry children in rags playing on streets
In cities away from the view of the wealthy,
Wearing the latest fashions and
Hiding weapons next to their chairs.
The more they have the more they want,
Piling millions onto millions. It's
Amazing they can live the way they do,
Importing exotic foods and wares from
Distant shores, eating till they burst, and
Searching out new ways to pass the time.
There are many robbers on the roadway,
But luxury is the worst of the lot.

The Way is mainly the road of compassion, and the most common route off the Way is clambering after money and riches. "It is hard for the rich to enter the kingdom of God" (Matt 19:23). Jesus told us: "Beware! Be on your guard against greed of every kind, for even when people have more than enough, wealth does not give them life" (Luke 12:15). It is the Way that gives life, and misuse of wealth too easily leads us away from that path.

The Foundation of the Way

A solid foundation is most important
For a building to stand tall and to last,
The reason a son praises his father
For living the long, good life.
When one person has integrity, strength can be seen;
When a family has integrity, strength multiplies;
When a village has integrity, strength adds weight;
When a country has integrity, strength attains greatness;
When the world has integrity, strength fills the skies;
Thus the integrity of one man
Seeds his family with the virtue,
And infuses the village as well,
And eventually uplifts the country
With the entire world to the skies.
This glorious happening could
All begin with me.

The foundation of the Way is Jesus, but his Way in the world depends on his believers, those who follow the path in him. "Believe in the light and you will become the children of the light, showing forth the fruit of the light" (Eph 5:8–9). Our foundation is strong but we need to depend on it to find the strength and integrity to share in building the kingdom of his Way. "We are his witnesses and so is the Holy Spirit" (Acts 5:32), each single one of us.

The Energy of the Spirit

When the glory of life
Infuses our spirit, even a
Child can withstand the poison
Of insects, the teeth of wild
Animals or vultures' bills.
A baby's grip can be as good as a man's,
Making even his sex organs respond to nature,
And he can scream all the day long
Without losing an ounce of energy
Because of the balance of spirit and life,
A balance all of us can achieve by
Living the Way of Life.
This is the most we can request from life,
We need not search for more.
We need not employ extraordinary
Efforts of will to attain greatness.
Let life ripen and fall.
Without the Way we can never truly live.

The Acts of the Apostles points to the power of the Spirit: "He has received from the Father the promised Holy Spirit and poured forth what you see and hear" (2:33)—"miracles, portents, signs, which God worked among you through him, as you well know" (2:22). This is the balance, energy, and joy the Spirit gives us when we do not allow our selfishness, or worries, or daily cares to interrupt the flow.

56

Uncluttering the Mind

If we know about the Way, we need not speak.
Those who do not know about it do all the talking.
The important thing is not to speak,
But rather to learn how to curb the tongue,
Not to scratch others with our barbs,
But to calm the waves of life.
When we maintain a clear-sighted view
And keep our mind uncluttered,
Our souls become balanced,
Beyond the impulses of love and hate,
Beyond the domination of profit or loss,
Or the disposition of praise or blame.
This is the highest, most elusive,
Goal of living.

The way of the world is "deception with smooth and flattering speech" (Rom 16:18), "gossiping and slandering" (Rom 1:29), and "seeking one's own glory" (John 7:18). Conversely, Jesus himself is our model of the Way, obedient to his Father in heaven, and living with compassion and integrity: his true legacy and power to those who become his followers.

57

The Use of Law

A country is governed by ordinary actions,
A battle is waged by extraordinary actions;
The world, properly governed,
Would need no actions at all.
How can I justify this statement?
This is how.
Government actions usually forbid
Everything except poverty, and
War generates nothing but madness,
And business leaves nothing but
Waste in its mad pursuit of profits.
Laws keep thieves and cheats active.
This is why I am driven to say that
If left to themselves, when we stop
Browbeating them, and pushing them
Around, and preaching to them,
People can take care of themselves.
That is how bad things are.

St. Paul tells us that "no one will be justified by works of the law" (Rom 3:20), and that "if you are led by the Spirit, you are not under the law" (Gal 5:18). Those who follow the Spirit in the Way, live in another dimension, outside the rules that others try to find ways to manipulate and bend. "The law is only our schoolteacher to bring us to Christ" (Gal 3:24) and his Way.

58

The Ways of the World

Politics has reached such a state that
We cannot bear to hear our leaders speak.
We are happier without their preaching,
And boasting, and strutting around the stage.
The fruits of their governments often
Lead to disaster and unhappiness, which
Ironically can help us understand what
Brings true happiness in this world. What is
Presented as happiness and success
Turns to unhappiness and disaster, and
The other way around. Fortunately
If our ideals do not demand what our
Leaders pretend to give, we can only
Stand above it all and simply ask for a

Semblance of honesty in their dealings.
We will then turn to a life that is opposite from
The one presented to us by officialdom,
One that is kind, and helpful, and personal.
Thus we may embody true leadership,
Showing the way people can lead each other.

"As the heavens are higher than the earth, so are God's ways above our ways" (Isa 55:9). We should not be surprised when the rules of society and government do not conform to the ideals of Christianity or other religions. "The path of the righteous is like the dawn" (Prov 4:18). That is, the Way is fleeting, uncertain, difficult to grasp, yet it is easy to understand that it is infinitely superior to the ways of the world. Our whole being tells us this is true.

59

Power of the Way

Only one force of the Way can inspire
The kind of leadership that doubles the
Strength of the strong, guides us
With the light of the heavens, keeps the
Weak from going astray, provides the
Greatest power of rebirth for the world and
Dynamo of life-giving infinite energy.
It is the Source of everything good and holy.

"God anointed Jesus with the Spirit and with power" (Acts 10:38). This same power is what lives in those who walk in his Way: "God has given us a Spirit of power" (2 Tim 1:7). Like St. Paul we are "striving according to his working which works in me in power" (Col 1:29). Our source, strength, dynamo, our power, our Way.

60

Gentleness

Every country should be governed gently,
As you would fry a small fish.
People have to be respected enough
To be left alone to live their lives
Without harassment or bother,
Lest their ghosts come back to haunt you.
This is entirely possible
Since only one force of life
Courses through everything dead or alive.

Gentleness is a signal characteristic of those who walk in the Way. "The wisdom from above is gentle" (Jas 3:17). When Jesus called himself "meek and humble of heart," this characteristic can be translated also as "gentle and humble-hearted" (Matt 11:29). Walking the gentle Way means that we treat others with respect and sensitivity. St. Paul explains, "We were as gentle as a nursing mother among you" (1 Thess 2:7).

61

Power and Covetousness

All countries, large and small,
Attract and repel one another,
Like positive and negative
Poles of a magnet.
They mindlessly seek their own
Advantage against the other,
Using their natural resources of
The earth or capital or cheap labor
Without regard for the needs of all people.
Large countries are more
Notorious for this habit than small.
If they would consider their weaker
Cousins as equal partners,
With compassion and understanding,
Each country could have what it needs.

*"From human nature and the heart come all kinds of coveting,"
Jesus warned us, "theft, murder, ruthless greed and deceit"
(Mark 7:21–23). And so we see these problems in the world
around us, in individuals, groups, and nations. These tendencies
are the polar opposite of living the Way of Life.*

62

The Good and the Bad

Life is sanctuary to everyone:
It harbors the good and the bad,
The talented and the simple,
Those who coast through it,
Those who connive in all their dealings,
And those who pay a heavy price for it.
Whether we pay a high premium
Or very little for our stay on earth,
It costs nothing to live a good life.
Yet none of us can take away the right
Of life from someone who is not good.
As the ancients said, "Only pursue an
Offender in order to show him the Way."
Because if we have received the gifts
Of life, and health, family, home,
And material gifts, along with integrity,
The least we can do is show compassion
To those who are not so blessed with
The greatest gift of all, the good life.

When St. Paul wrote to the Corinthians, he made a point of reminding them that they were all at different levels of growth in Christ: "At first I could not speak to you as I should speak to people who have the Spirit. I had to deal with you on the merely natural plane at first. . . . Can you not see that while there is jealousy and strife among you, you are living on the purely human level of your lower nature?" (1 Cor 3:1–3). The good and the bad live together, while even those living with the Spirit are on different levels of life in Christ.

63

Building God's House

Those who practice the Way of Life
Conduct their affairs without
Self-consciousness, act without
Forcing their desires, can even
Taste without touching a morsel,
So filled are they with the Spirit.
Meeting many people they can
Touch the few; they find great souls
Among the humble;
They can respect their enemies, and
Deal with a situation before it becomes
Complicated, and solve a small problem
Before it turns into a nightmare.
The most trying problem in the world
Could have been faced when it was simple.
In fact, the biggest problem in the world
Could have been solved when it was small.
Because spiritually healthy people find
No problems unwieldy, they are successful.
They are not quick with a yes or a no, and
Therefore do not have to change their answers.
They know that no problem is easily solved,
So they calmly solve both the easy and the
Difficult: they know how to face troubles with
Serenity, so no problems trouble them.

We live in the world as "God's fellow workers and as God's garden and God's building.... But there can be no other foundation beyond that which is already laid; I mean Jesus Christ himself.... Surely you know you are God's Temple where the Spirit of God dwells.... We must be regarded as Christ's underlings and as stewards of the secrets of God" (1 Cor 3:9, 11, 17; 4:1). This is the reason those filled with the Spirit can do great and wonderful works.

64

Problem Solving and the Spirit

Before something moves, grab it,
Before something goes wrong,
Form it according to its nature.
Don't wait for the winter freeze
Before you drain off the water,
Pull weeds from your garden before they
Kill your plants. You can foresee
Many problems before they happen
And nip them in the bud.
A gigantic redwood tree begins with a seed,
The tallest high-rise from a building block,
A thousand-mile walk starts with one step.
Act too fast, and you might hurt someone.
When you grasp impulsively, you lose.
Spiritually healthy people think before
They act lest they miss their mark or
Cause personal harm and damage.
When people are impetuous and lose
Because of this fault, they should have
Known the outcome from the start.
Healthy people know they don't have
To work from dawn to dusk, don't have to
Crave what most of the world craves, don't
Have to possess the latest gadgets.
Society might call them laggards, but
These healthy people of few words are
Interested mostly in not interfering with

The course of nature, but rather letting it flow
In the direction society seems determined
To disturb.

"The fruits of the Spirit are love, joy, patience, kindness, serenity, gentleness, self-control" (Gal 5:22) says St. Paul, echoing the proverb, "He who restrains his words has a cool spirit" (Prov 17:27). Those who live with these gifts and a "cool spirit" can solve daily problems without stress, without wear and tear. Their secret is the "cool" Spirit who infuses their problem-solving activity.

65

Wisdom of the Way

Governments need to trust the people
Instead of deciding what's good for them,
Or deciding for them what they should know.
The country has to be established in a way
That enables us to think for ourselves,
To know that we don't know, or that
We understand more than we know,
To see that we are dependent
Upon each other for the good of all.
These should be the goals of government,
To help us find wisdom and vision
In every corner of our common life.

Those who govern assume that their laws embody wisdom and truth. When St. Paul spoke about wisdom, he said, "Make no mistake about this: If there is anyone among you who fancies himself wise—wise, I mean by the standards of this passing age—he must become a fool to gain wisdom. For although everything belongs to you—the world, life, and death, the present and the future, all of them belong to you—yet you belong to Christ and Christ to God" (1 Cor 3:18–23). If governments and people would cultivate the true wisdom to deal with daily problems, they need to cultivate the Source of true wisdom.

66

Humble Leadership

Why do we admire and respect the
Great seas of the world? Because they
Coalesce on one great common level.
We also respect spiritually healthy
Leaders because they do not consider
Themselves on a higher level than others,
Because although they may lead us,
They also follow us, they do not
Push or pull us, do not weigh
Heavily upon us. And because
They do not put shackles on us,
We are happy to have them lead:
We never tire of those who don't
Demean any of our number.

*Like the great seas of the world, which automatically know that
they have to seek a common level, Christians are told "to live
with humility and gentleness" (Eph 4:2). Early Christians
referred to themselves as* anawim, *or "poor in spirit," imitating
Jesus who "emptied himself" to live a common human life.
Therefore when the followers of his Way "humble themselves
they are exalted" because they see themselves as one with him
and other humans.*

67

Living the Way

I don't know why but everyone
Thinks the way I live my life is silly and
Idiotic, but the way of an idiot is just
What makes my life worthwhile.
If it were not idiotic, it would be
Worthless. I need only three
Possessions to hold and cherish:
To care about others,
To be fair to everyone,
To be humble in the Way.
When we care, we carry no fear,
When we are fair, we want
Others to have enough to live on,
When we are humble, we continue
To grow in the life of the Way.
If we act like those who are
Brash without caring,
Self-indulgent without sharing,
Proud of achievements without
Recognizing the efforts of others,
We are dead, an empty shell.
Only caring can completely shield us
From dying the death of the damned.

When Jesus said, "I am the Way" (John 14:6), he was also telling us, in the words of Isaiah, "This is the way, walk in it" (Isa 30:21). When the early Christians referred to their new religion as "the Way" *(Acts 9:2; 19:9, 23; 24:14, 22)*, they meant that they should follow Jesus in his "Way" of caring, gentleness, fairness, and humility.

Fellowship and Tolerance

The best leader does not thoughtlessly
Charge into battle, nor does the best
Soldier always itch for a fight.
The real winner is the one who wins
Without any fight at all.
We need to understand those whom
We want to win over to our side.
Our serenity prevails when we shed
The stress of rivalry and competition.
As the ancients have said,
Fellowship with heaven means
Fellowship with humans.
The adage will always hold true.

All humans share a common humanity and thus should share fellowship and tolerance for each other. To emphasize this, Christians believe we have a special "fellowship with God" (1 John 1:6) because we share a "fellowship with his Son" (1 Cor 1:9). With this common humanity, and a fellowship with heaven, our first human impulse should be one of affection and tolerance. We need to see that all of us have a common origin, common needs, and a common future in God. Human conflict is its antithesis.

Loving Enemies

Handbooks on self-defense say,
"Never look for a fight but
Accept it if you have to."
"It's better to be an hour late for an
Opponent than to be a minute early."
That means: Look him straight in the
Eye, but don't move on him.
Be ready, but don't clench your fists.
Show open hands, that you have no
Weapon, nothing under your sleeve.
Do not consider him the enemy,
But value him as another human,
Respect and try to understand him.
However strong he may be,
Don't let him take your compassion
From you, for that is your
Most precious advantage.

With revolutionary fervor, Jesus said to his disciples, "You have learned the lesson, 'Love your neighbor, hate your enemy.' But what I tell you is this: Love your enemies and pray for your persecutors; only this way can you be children of your heavenly Father, who makes his sun rise on good and bad alike, and sends the rain on the honest and the dishonest" (Matt 5:43–45). We who are slow to fight and quick to forgive become "all goodness just as our heavenly Father is good" (Matt 5:48).

70

Simplicity of the Way

The reason so many people do not try
The Way is that it is so easy and simple.
If it were not universal and natural,
If it were flimsy and artificial,
Everyone would want to try it.
Yet however few desire to practice
The Way, the wise will understand
What they see before them, that
Sanity and spiritual health are
Rough clothing hiding a precious jewel.

*Jesus often tried to tell his followers that his Way is easy and
simple, so much so that even the most unsophisticated can quickly
understand its meaning: "I thank you, Father, Lord of heaven*

and earth, for hiding these things from the learned, and revealing them to the simple" (Matt 11:25). The learned often have difficulty seeing into the heart of the matter.

Becoming Spiritually Well

People who know how little they know are healthy,
People who think they know it all are sick,
When you see the symptoms,
When you know what makes you sick,
You should act quickly,
Because you also know the cure.

St. Paul describes the spiritually healthy followers of Christ as "reflecting as in a mirror the splendor of the Lord; thus we are transfigured into his likeness, from splendor to splendor; such is the influence of the Lord who is Spirit" (2 Cor 3:18). Our deepest health is shown forth in our union with the Spirit of Christ. Symptoms of spiritual sickness—mean-spiritedness and hard-heartedness—need to be quickly recognized and eliminated.

72

Authority Within

Authority is the means society
Uses to control its population.
Ignoring authority does not mean
People are either good or bad,
Whether or not they are punished
For their insubordination.
Healthy people do not need
Authority figures to tell them
What to do, but only knowledge of
Themselves, self-esteem, and humility.
We do not need to show how strong
We are if our muscles are well developed.

*In his epistle to the Romans, St. Paul shows that external
human laws "multiplied lawbreaking, but grace immeasurably
exceeded it, so that God's grace might establish its reign in
eternal life through Jesus Christ our Lord. . . . In the same way
you must regard yourself as dead to sin and alive to God, in
union with Christ Jesus" (Rom 5:20–21; 6:11). Human laws
are insignificant when compared to the inner law of the Way in
Christ Jesus.*

73

Ethical Quandaries

Who is to say which virtue is greater:
The person with physical courage
Who is willing to die for a cause,
Or the person with spiritual courage
Who is willing to live the good life?
Both have good points to consider.
Could any of us tell which one
Heaven would prefer?
Eternity doesn't tip its hand,
But is echoed in the world.
It never passes down clear-cut orders,
Yet always accomplishes its goals,
Nor does it offer advice,
But is always right.
And who of us, seeing that heaven
Casts its wide net over all things,
Could ever figure out
How it is cast.

The life of Jesus shows many examples where he had to make ethical decisions about right and wrong; sometimes two or more courses of action were good, but one was superior. "How will you understand all the parables?" (Mark 4:13) Jesus asked his followers. He demonstrated that there are alternative ways to walk the Way, that "heaven casts a wide net over many things," in the words of the Tao.

Capital Punishment

Death cannot be a threat to
Criminals who are not afraid to die;
But even if they were quaking with
Fear, who would dare take the role
Of executioner? Nature should be
The executioner, not human beings.
When we take a human life,
We are like a carpenter's apprentice
Who thinks he is a master.
"An apprentice wielding the master's
Axe may well hack his own hand in half."

The closest Jesus comes to recommending death for any action was his condemnation of someone who leads children away from his teaching: that "it would be better to have a millstone hung around his neck and he be drowned in the depths of the sea" (Matt 18:6). Regarding capital punishment, his own life is more instructive. He did not kill his enemies who threatened his own life, or recommend his followers to take up arms on his behalf. Instead he taught forgiveness, caring, and love of enemies.

75

True Authority

If a nation cannot work for food,
If taxes are so heavy the people starve,
The leaders must take the blame
For all the hunger, pain, and death.
Revolution is the consequence of
This state of affairs, for starving
People are not afraid to die.
They win because their leaders
Are fat and do not want to die.

In the world of human society, some assume authority for the common good, but as Jesus reminds us, it is a provisional authority based on a greater law: "You would have no authority at all if it were not given to you from above," he tells Pilate (John 19:11). Leaders must look out for the welfare of all the people, strive for the common good, serve in everyone's interest. Christians need to be aware of a law not constrained by the marketplace or the interests of politicians.

Gentle or Hardened Souls

Babes are soft and yielding,
The old taken in death
Become stiff and brittle.
We are flexible as we grow
Until we are dead in the grave.
But many people also harden
During their lives as "death's kin,"
While the softly gentle are "life's kin."
Hardened armies can never win.
Hardened trees are cut down.
When the tough and stiff die,
The young, soft sprig appears.

The Bible speaks of the Pharaoh and Israel hardening their hearts with a variety of sins. "Jesus reproached them for their hardness of heart"(Mark 16:14), and preached gentleness and goodness throughout his ministry. The Way is essentially one of gentleness and love, not hardness and conflict, which are physical signs of death.

The Rich Society

May we compare true living
To a pulled and drawn bow?
The tips come closer together,
The length becomes shorter,
The width becomes more narrow.
In a just society the length of
Wealth would be narrowed to
Help those with too little,
Yet very often the opposite is
What happens in real life.
Spiritually healthy people know
That Nature offers all of us
Common gifts that we should
Share together. These should
Not be taken from us,
For in them we find
A deep, fulfilling equality.

Though Jesus tells us that "it is hard for the rich to enter into the kingdom of God" or that "a rich man ended up in hell" (Luke 18:24; 16:22–23), the New Testament instructs individuals and does not speak specifically about the duties of society toward the common good. Yet Christian teaching implies that we can show our love of neighbor effectively by working through communities of interest and government bodies.

78

The Power of Love

We all know that water is soft and
Yielding as it slips through our fingers.
It also can wear down the hardest
Boulders along the stream.
This is how the most tender of
The weak can wear down the strong,
And the humble overcome the proud.
Why can't we learn this lesson?
Because the compassionate seem to be weak
And the high and mighty seem strong.

*God's love for his people is the major theme of the Bible: "Who
did not spare his own Son, but surrendered him for us all. . . .
Then what can separate us from the love of Christ? Can afflic-
tion or hardship? Can persecution, hunger, nakedness, peril, or
the sword?. . . Nothing in all creation can separate us from the
love of God in Christ Jesus our Lord" (Rom 8:32, 35, 38–39).
Love, like water, which seems so weak and soft, is the most
powerful force on earth because it is the essence of God.*

79

Beyond Justice

If we settle a dispute with
Terms that leave a bad taste,
What good are they?
A good man may accept terms
That are not favorable to him
Without making a fuss about it,
Rather than cloud the future
Of a relationship or business.
Sometimes it pays to forego
Justice for the good of harmony.
Justice is for earthly actions,
Harmony is a heavenly thing.

Jesus went out of his way to show the Pharisees that the strict justice of the law does not define human relationships. "One Sabbath he went to have a meal in the house of a leading Pharisee; and they were watching him closely" (Luke 14:1). He cured a man suffering from dropsy—not permitted by the law on the Sabbath—and reported that his followers avoided the law of the Sabbath on hundreds of things regularly with no complaints from the Pharisees. Common sense inspired by compassion supersedes the law in Christianity as well as in daily life.

80

The Good Life

If the people live in a country rich
In natural goods and activities,
And if they have not learned how
To waste their goods and culture,
They will so love their country
That no weapon, not even wild tigers,
Could drive them from their homes.
People know when they are well off,
Eating plain food, wearing common clothes
And living in simple, well-made houses.
Their villages might even be close enough
That they hear the barking dogs of one other,
But they realize that they are so comfortable
With their lives that leaving home never
Even enters their minds.
Where would they go that could be better?

Jesus and the Tao paint similar pictures of the good life: living in harmony with nature and one another; sharing the goods of the world "content with what they have" (Luke 3:14; Heb 13:5). Stressing love, Jesus said, "Where your treasure is, there will your heart be also" (Matt 6:21). Jesus' life was one of simplicity, sharing meals with friends, enemies, and outcasts alike. He found nothing or no one to be unworthy of him since all creation comes from God. The gentle, contented life was his ideal.

81

Simplicity and Innocence

Solid words are not prideful,
Prideful words are not solid;
And because arguments never
Prove anything, sensible people
Prefer not to argue.
Spiritually healthy people are wiser
Than they think; silly people think
They know more than they do.
Therefore spiritually healthy people
Are not interested in pretense.
The more they serve others,
The more others want to help them;
The more they are yielding to others,
The more others yield to them.

Spiritually healthy people embody
The Way. They know that being
Is more important than acting.

"At that time the disciples came to Jesus and asked, 'Who is the greatest in the kingdom of heaven?' He called a child, set him in front of them, and said, 'I tell you this: Unless you turn round and become like children, you will never enter the kingdom of Heaven. Let a man humble himself till he is like this child, and he will be the greatest in the kingdom of Heaven'" (Matt 18:1–4). Children are simple, accepting, yielding, do not construct arguments to prove their case, do not pretend, and seek to please. It is not the role of Christians to crush others, or prove anything to them, but to serve them with simplicity.

The Tao Te Ching
and Christianity

What we know of the legend of Lao Tzu, the reputed author of the *Tao Te Ching*, comes from Ssu-ma Ch'ien (145–86 B.C.E.), who tells us that Lao Tzu was so disgusted with the legalisms of the contemporary Confucian society, which he believed were destroying religious sensitivity, that he fled to the wilderness to live out his life as a hermit. Although Confucius lived in the sixth and fifth centuries B.C.E., many other religious recluses predated Lao Tzu by a few hundred years in the same north central region of China. They might have eventually become a loosely organized religious clan and developed the kind of religious sayings found in the *Tao Te Ching*. Nonetheless, Ssu-ma Ch'ien gave the book its title, credits Lao Tzu—who is said to have been born in 604 B.C.E.—as the author, and tells us that on his way west to the back country, Lao Tzu was asked by an official at the frontier to write him a book about his teachings. Lao Tzu, Ch'ien claims, obliged him with a book of about five thousand words.

Whether the *Tao Te Ching* was written by one person in the sixth century B.C.E. or by many people over the centuries before and after Lao Tzu, it remains a book of marvelous internal integrity and coherence and one that has had a strong influence on people around the world for hundreds of years. It can be read by our age as easily as it was more than two thousand years ago, because its central concept is that the universe is governed by the one Spirit, powerful and compassionate, whose principle is the supreme model and force of all natural being. The ideas resonate not only within the great religions of the world, but also with famous philosophers: Aristotle, Plato, Socrates, Marcus Aurelius, Thomas Aquinas, Spinoza, Bergson, Teilhard de Chardin, and countless others.

Even more relevant to passing ages have been the author's mysticism and pragmatic morality. He believed that because of our inherent spiritual nature, all of us can find goodness and happiness within ourselves if we are only willing to acknowledge that reality and live according to it. The fact of a common spiritual nature also underlines why all people deserve respect and compassion. This is the major theme of Lao Tzu's writing; it occurs within a framework of marvelous ethical inspiration and practical advice. If this major theme were its only connection with Christianity, it would be a powerful one. What makes its relevance extraordinary are the many related ideas that coalesce so easily between the two world views.

In the very first chapter we are introduced to the nature of God and the world. There we learn that the ultimate Being or Spirit is nameless and indescribable yet embraces all being. In fact nothing can be separated from It as It is Wonder Itself. As God proclaims to Moses in Exodus, "I am who am." In Genesis we are told that humans are created in the image and likeness of God; in the New Testament we are identified with Jesus, who is one with the Father.

Tao, as the first word in the book's title, means "Way,"

and that word is overflowing with meaning. The Chinese character is composed of the head of a human combined with a primitive depiction of walking. Its simplest sense is a path, but to Chinese mystics it referred to "the Way" as the eternal pattern and model of the universe: the way it operates. At the same time that Lao Tzu lived, Heraclitus of Ephesus wrote that a *logos*—or pattern, model, and order—organizes the universe and all of nature so that the world is not hopelessly disrupted by continual change.

At the beginning of the Gospel of St. John we read, "In the beginning was the Word, and the Word was with God, and the Word was God." "Word" is translated from that same Greek *logos*, which refers to the idea behind the word: a way or a pattern and model of all reality, for the Word is made flesh. Later in John, Jesus says "I am the Way." He is the Way and the Word, an eternal pattern, model, and human example, living the divine life which supports all reality. He speaks the Word of the Father, the Truth; is One with the Father; and is the Word, the Way which abides in his followers as eternal life and gives them the power to follow the Way.

In the Acts of the Apostles, Christianity is described simply as "the Way," meaning the Way of the Lord or the Way of God. That is, it is more than a set of propositions or code of moral prescriptions, such as the multiple laws of their Jewish forebears, or the endless ethical rules of Confucius. It is Jesus himself, who is also the Truth and the Life, who resides in his believers. Thus, the Way, or Tao, the eternal pattern living in all things of the universe of the Chinese mystics, is given a face and a life for Christians. For Christians the supreme goal of life is union or identification with Christ. For Taoist mystics the supreme goal of life is union or identification with Tao.

Te or *Teh* refers to virtue, character, influence, moral force. The Chinese character has three parts: one meaning "to go," the second meaning "straight," and the third, a picturograph meaning "the heart." The whole character refers to pure internal motivation and outward character. Blakney quotes a second-century Chinese dictionary (referring to older authorities) defining *Te* as "the outward effect of a man and the inward effect of the self." That which inspires this effect is the Way. *Ching* means "classic," so *Tao Te Ching* means "The Classic Text of the Way and Its Virtue," popularly known as "The Way of Life." The New Testament likewise could be called, "The Classic Text of Jesus Christ and His Way of Life." In both cases, the written text provides a set of practical ideas for living, as well as the power and inspiration to live those ideas.

To groups around the world throughout history, especially in China, "virtue" or "power" resided in people and things. It enabled them to perform quasi-magical acts. In Lao Tzu the word "virtue" also implies a moral force, as in chapter 67 where we are told that if we follow the Way, we are able to develop the virtues of caring, fairness, and humility. In the gospels Jesus feels virtue or power flowing from him when he heals the sick, and in John it was the Holy Spirit, sent in Jesus' name, who would transform his disciples as they followed the Way.

One of the most discussed phrases of the Tao, also a central Buddhist concept, is *wei wu wei*, which means "to act without acting." *Wei* usually means to act or do something, and *wu* is a negative, thus the phrase literally means "act not acting." The Taoist principle is based on the way nature is seeded, grows, lives, and dies without putting up any obstacles, allowing the divine principle to work through it. Lao Tzu advises us in many different ways that it is "more important to be than to act," since the world is Tao's work. At the same time the author never tires of exhorting us to follow the Way within us. So the first *wei* is the Way or divine principle; *wu wei* is human activity. The idea is to let the divine pass through us without hindering the process, even though "not hindering" sometimes requires significant will power, as in allowing the divine life of Jesus to enlighten, inspire, and work through us.

The phrase is one expression of the religious sentiment that acknowledges God's will and God's mysterious ways of acting in the world, that we must learn to accept what we cannot change and above all to acknowledge that it is God who is the ultimate Reality and Principle of Life. In the gospels the meaning is found in "Consider the lilies of the field, how they grow, they neither sow nor reap." Acceptance of God's will while choosing to live the life of the Way is the Christian's "acting without acting." With Lao Tzu we can say, "Existence never presents itself with perfect clarity. Words are too frail to describe the depth of its Reality" (chapter 1), but we freely accept it and will live our lives according to its pattern or Way.

An allied term of *wei wu wei,* and a symbol of "The Way and Its Virtue," is the character *P'o.* It is a type of tree that remains untouched, therefore a virgin standing piece of wood, not made into an object, not artificial. It is the natural state of things in raw material form. It refers to the mystics' desire to fully live the divine life without the corruption of civilization and its artificial manners. A similar term is *pu shi*, "to stay independent of the world," uninvolved with anything that takes one away from living the Way. It is the heart of the mystical life.

Lao Tzu often uses the term *Sheng Jen. Sheng* means the duty to listen (to the power within) and then say what one has heard. *Jen* is a person and refers to the wise person or spiritually healthy people because they can hear the voice of the Way (or the Word of God) and act on it, as in "he who hears the Word of God (Way) is of God" (John 8:47). *Sheng Jen* is used sixty times in the *Tao Te Ching*.

The term for God or the heavens or sky is *T'ien*. The term is personal in Lao Tzu, even though the translation may refer to the heavens. It goes together with nature and Way. The Way is God's Way, and it is nature's Way, but it is also personal, since humans are involved. That is, God or the Way is not some impersonal force. Since humans are personal, the Greater Being must also be personal, so the mystic can communicate with that Source which is the Way. The Way of nature is dynamic, a movement, an effortless rhythm like the change of seasons. Yet in the *Tao* and especially in Christianity, God or the Way is personal, even in its exhortations to follow the Way of nature, because the divine life within it is the same as the divine life within us all.

In the *Tao Te Ching*—like many ancient texts, including the Bible—the sayings of people of wisdom are sprinkled, undoubtedly many more than are found in quotation marks. These sayings and stories not only tell their readers how to live successful lives, but also how to be free from anxiety that comes from hostility, competition, opposition, and failure. They were discussed and written down by a class of scribes in official palaces and temples and taught to the young boys who would be their successors. Many sages went beyond matters of conduct and dealt with problems of good and evil, of the success of wickedness and the failure of righteousness, as did the writers of Job and Ecclesiastes. Solomon's wisdom uses nature to teach a way of life, and wisdom literature in the Bible also emphasizes that wisdom is ultimately a gift from Yahweh. Jesus himself "grew in wisdom," and acquaintances wondered where he had acquired it. Jesus promises his disciples "mouth and wisdom," and the wisdom of God which speaks in Luke 11:49 is a paraphrase for God himself. The *Tao Te Ching* is a parallel text in teaching wisdom to wise people, or "spiritually healthy" people, that is, those who are willing to accept and practice The Way of Life.

Those who read the *Tao Te Ching* continually come upon texts that are paraphrases of those in the gospels. For example:

Can you become as simple as a child? (Ch. 10)

Unless you are converted and become as little children, you shall not enter the kingdom of God. (Matt 18:3)

Those who use force will die the death. (Ch. 42)

Those who take the sword will perish by the sword. (Matt 26:52)

Which is more dear to you, you or your reputation? Which means more to you, you or your possessions? (Ch. 44)

What shall it profit a man if he gain the whole world and suffer the loss of his soul? (Matt 16:26)

We would find good people good, and even find bad people good. (Ch. 49)

Love your enemies, bless those who curse you, do good to those who hate you, and pray for those who spitefully use you and persecute you. (Matt 5:44)

When we care, we carry no fear. (Ch. 67)

Blessed are the merciful, for they shall obtain mercy. (Matt 5:7)

The Way is easy and simple. (Ch. 70)

My yoke is easy and my burden light. (Matt 11:30)

Hardened trees are cut down. When the tough and stiff die, the young, soft sprig appears. (Ch. 76)

Everyone who exults himself shall be humbled, he who humbles himself shall be exulted. (Luke 18:14)

The promise and hope of the *Tao Te Ching* are optimistic and challenging. At the very end of the book, in chapter 80, the image is one of a happy and comfortable life in a small town, something like what environmentalists are calling for in a sustainable society. In chapter 54, the author wants to teach us that a spiritually healthy social order is possible because "it can start with me." At the bottom of all prospects, however, is the power of the Way, whether we are referring to the Tao or Jesus Christ. Although practitioners of the Tao and Buddhism from the East and many of their followers from the West think of Eastern religions as becoming engrossed in the Great Void or the impersonal God, a closer examination of the Tao shows the close connection between the power of God in the universe and his loving kindness as a personal God through the face and life of Jesus Christ himself.